Building Secure Web Applications with Blockchain and Web3 Technology

I0012236

About the book

"Building Secure Web Applications with Blockchain and Web3 Technology" is a comprehensive guide designed to help developers, security professionals, and tech enthusiasts understand how to leverage blockchain and Web3 technology for building safer, more secure web applications. This book covers essential topics like blockchain fundamentals, smart contracts, decentralized identity management, and user authentication, all while addressing Web3 security threats and best practices. With practical insights on blockchain-based data storage, security auditing, and regulatory compliance, this book is a must-read for anyone looking to enhance the security of their web apps in the era of Web3. Whether you're a beginner or an expert, you'll gain valuable knowledge to protect your digital assets, prevent hacking, and ensure privacy in today's decentralized web. Designed for a global audience, this book serves as the definitive resource for anyone looking to understand the future of Web3 security.

Author

Table of Contents

Chapter 1: Blockchain Fundamentals

Chapter 2: Blockchain Security Features

Chapter 3: Web3 Security Threats

Chapter 4: Blockchain-Based User Authentication

Chapter 5: Blockchain-Based Data Storage

Chapter 6: Blockchain-Based Smart Contracts

Chapter 7: Blockchain-Based Identity Management

Chapter 8: Web3 Security Best Practices

Chapter 9: Web3 Security Tools and Resources

Chapter 10: Web3 Security Auditing

Chapter 11: Web3 Threat Intelligence

Chapter 12: Web3 Incident Response

Chapter 13: Web3 Regulatory Compliance

Chapter 14: Web3 Security Research

Chapter 15: The Future of Web3 Security

Chapter 1: Blockchain Fundamentals

Introduction

Blockchain technology is a distributed ledger technology (DLT) that allows for secure, transparent, and tamper-proof transactions. It is the underlying technology behind cryptocurrencies, such as Bitcoin and Ethereum, but it has many other potential applications in a wide range of industries.

Distributed Ledger Technology (DLT)

A distributed ledger is a database that is shared and synchronized across multiple computers. This means that there is no single point of failure, and the data is very difficult to tamper with. Blockchain is a type of DLT that uses cryptography to secure the data and ensure its authenticity.

Consensus Mechanisms

One of the key features of blockchain technology is its use of consensus mechanisms. A consensus mechanism is a way to ensure that all participants in a blockchain network agree on the state of the ledger. There are a number of different consensus mechanisms, such as proof-of-work (PoW) and proof-of-stake (PoS).

Smart Contracts

Smart contracts are self-executing contracts that are stored on a blockchain. They can be used to automate a wide range of transactions, such as supply chain management, financial transactions, and voting.

Unique Examples of Blockchain Technology in Action

Here are a few unique examples of how blockchain technology is being used today:

- Provenance: Provenance is a blockchain-based platform that tracks the supply chain of goods. This allows consumers to see where their food and other products come from and to ensure that they are ethically sourced.

- Everledger: Everledger is a blockchain-based platform that tracks the ownership of diamonds. This helps to prevent fraud and ensure that diamonds are not conflict-free.

- VeChain: VeChain is a blockchain-based platform that tracks the movement of goods through a supply chain. This helps to improve transparency and efficiency.

Real-Time Practical Business Case Studies

Here are a few real-time practical business case studies of how blockchain technology is being used by businesses today:

- Walmart: Walmart is using blockchain technology to track the food supply chain. This helps to improve food safety and reduce waste.

- Maersk: Maersk is using blockchain technology to streamline its shipping operations. This has helped to reduce costs and improve efficiency.

- JPMorgan Chase: JPMorgan Chase is using blockchain technology to develop a new payment system called JPM Coin. This system is designed to enable faster and more efficient payments between banks.

Benefits of Blockchain Technology

Blockchain technology offers a number of benefits, including:

- Security: Blockchain technology is very secure, thanks to its use of cryptography and consensus mechanisms.

- Transparency: Blockchain technology is very transparent, as all transactions are recorded on the public ledger.

- Efficiency: Blockchain technology can help to improve the efficiency of many business processes.

- Trustlessness: Blockchain technology can help to reduce the need for trust between parties, as all transactions are verified by the network.

Challenges of Blockchain Technology

Blockchain technology is still a relatively new technology, and there are a number of challenges that need to be addressed before it can be widely adopted. These challenges include:

- Scalability: Current blockchain networks can only process a limited number of transactions per second. This needs to be improved before blockchain can be used for high-volume applications.

- Regulation: There is currently no clear regulatory framework for blockchain technology. This could hinder its adoption by businesses.

- Education: There is a lack of awareness and understanding of blockchain technology among businesses and consumers. This needs to be addressed before blockchain can be widely adopted.

Conclusion

Blockchain technology is a powerful new technology with the potential to revolutionize many industries. However, it is still a relatively new technology, and there are a number of challenges that need to be addressed before it can be widely adopted.

Chapter 2: Blockchain Security Features

Introduction

Blockchain security is essential for ensuring the integrity and reliability of these applications. There are a number of features built into blockchain technology that contribute to its security, including cryptography, decentralization, and immutability.

Cryptography

Cryptography is the use of mathematical algorithms to protect data from unauthorized access, use, disclosure, disruption, modification, or destruction. Blockchain uses cryptography to secure data at multiple levels, including:

- Transaction encryption: Transactions are encrypted before they are added to the blockchain, making them unreadable to anyone without the appropriate decryption keys. This helps to protect the privacy of sensitive data, such as financial transactions or medical records.

- Digital signatures: Digital signatures are used to authenticate transactions and prevent them from being tampered with. When a user initiates a transaction, they sign it with their private key. This signature is then verified by all nodes on the network before the transaction is added to the blockchain.

- Hashing: Hashing is a cryptographic function that converts data of any size into a fixed-size string of characters. Blockchain uses hashing to create a unique identifier for each block in the chain. This makes it very difficult to tamper with or remove blocks from the blockchain without being detected.

Decentralization

Decentralization is another key security feature of blockchain. A decentralized blockchain is one that is not controlled by any single entity. Instead, it is maintained by a network of computers (nodes) that are distributed all over the world.

This makes blockchain very resistant to attack. If one node is compromised, it cannot affect the rest of the network. Additionally, it is very difficult to take down a decentralized blockchain because it would require compromising a majority of the nodes on the network.

Immutability

Immutability refers to the fact that data on a blockchain is very difficult to change or delete. Once a block is added to the blockchain, it cannot be removed or altered without the consensus of the majority of the nodes on the network.

This makes blockchain ideal for storing important records, such as financial transactions, property titles, and healthcare records. It also makes blockchain very resistant to fraud and tampering.

Examples of Blockchain Security Features in Action

Here are a few examples of how blockchain security features are being used in the real world:

- Supply chain management: Blockchain is being used to track the movement of goods through supply chains. This helps to ensure that products are authentic and that they have not been tampered with. For example, the IBM Food Trust network uses blockchain to track the movement of food from farm to fork. This helps to ensure that food is safe and that it meets quality standards.

- Voting systems: Blockchain is being used to develop secure and transparent voting systems. For example, the Voatz app allows users to vote on their smartphones using blockchain technology. This makes it easier for people to vote and helps to reduce the risk of fraud.

- Healthcare records: Blockchain is being used to store and share healthcare records securely. This helps to improve the quality of care and gives patients more control over their own data. For example, the MedRec blockchain platform allows patients to store their medical records securely and share them with authorized healthcare providers.

Real-Time Practical Business Case Studies

Here are a few real-time practical business case studies of how blockchain security features are being used in businesses today:

- Everledger: Everledger is a company that uses blockchain to track the provenance of diamonds. This helps to ensure that diamonds are ethically sourced and that they are not counterfeit. Everledger's customers include major diamond producers and retailers, such as De Beers and Tiffany & Co.

- Provenance: Provenance is a company that uses blockchain to track the supply chains of food and other products. This helps to ensure that products are authentic and that they have not been tampered with. Provenance's customers include major food brands, such as Nestlé and Unilever.

- VeChain: VeChain is a company that uses blockchain to track the supply chains of luxury goods. This helps to ensure that luxury goods are authentic and that they have not been counterfeited. VeChain's customers include major luxury brands, such as LVMH and BMW.

Conclusion

Blockchain security features are essential for ensuring the integrity and reliability of blockchain-based applications. By using cryptography, decentralization, and immutability, blockchain technology can provide a high level of security for sensitive data and transactions.

Blockchain security features are already being used in a variety of real-world applications, and their adoption is expected to grow in the coming years. As blockchain technology continues to mature and become more widely adopted, we can expect to see even more innovative and groundbreaking uses of blockchain security features. For example, blockchain is being explored for use in areas such as:

- Identity management: Blockchain can be used to create secure and tamper-proof digital identities. This could help to reduce fraud and identity theft.

- Digital rights management: Blockchain can be used to protect the copyrights and intellectual property rights of digital content creators.

- Regulatory compliance: Blockchain can be used to help businesses comply with regulations, such as those related to anti-money laundering and know-your-customer requirements.

Overall, blockchain security features offer a number of potential benefits for businesses and consumers alike. By making it possible to securely share and exchange data without the need for a trusted third party, blockchain can help to build trust and transparency in a variety of industries.

Chapter 3: Web3 Security Threats

Introduction

Web3, also known as the decentralized web, represents a paradigm shift in how the internet operates. Built on blockchain technology, it aims to provide greater control, transparency, and security for users while eliminating intermediaries. However, this shift towards a decentralized model also introduces new security challenges that must be addressed to ensure the integrity of Web3 applications. In this topic, we will discuss some of the unique security threats that Web3 applications face, including smart contract vulnerabilities, phishing attacks, and supply chain attacks. Real-time practical business case studies will be analyzed to provide insight into the latest developments and trends in Web3 security.

I. Smart Contract Vulnerabilities

Smart contracts are self-executing agreements with the terms of the contract directly written into code. These contracts play a critical role in Web3 applications, automating processes, enabling decentralized finance (DeFi) platforms, and more. However, they are not immune to vulnerabilities. Some of the most common smart contract vulnerabilities include:

Reentrancy Attacks

Reentrancy attacks occur when a malicious contract can repeatedly call a target contract, interrupting its execution and causing it to behave unexpectedly. This can result in the unauthorized transfer of assets or denial of service. One real-time case study of a reentrancy attack is the DAO (Decentralized Autonomous Organization) incident in 2016. A hacker exploited a vulnerability in the DAO smart contract, draining over $60 million in Ether.

Integer Overflow and Underflow

Smart contracts often involve arithmetic operations, and if not implemented carefully, they can lead to integer overflow or underflow vulnerabilities. In 2020, the dForce DeFi platform was exploited due to an integer overflow bug, resulting in the theft of $25 million in cryptocurrency.

Uninitialized Storage

An uninitialized storage vulnerability occurs when a smart contract fails to properly initialize critical variables, potentially allowing an attacker to manipulate these variables and compromise the contract's functionality. A real-world example of this vulnerability was discovered in the Augur prediction market platform, which could have enabled an attacker to manipulate markets.

Time Manipulation

Smart contracts often rely on timestamps, which can be manipulated by miners or external actors. This can lead to various forms of attack, such as front-running or other malicious activities. While not a specific example, the potential for time manipulation remains a prevalent threat in the Web3 ecosystem.

II. Phishing Attacks

Phishing attacks in the context of Web3 refer to fraudulent attempts to trick users into revealing their private keys, mnemonic phrases, or other sensitive information. These attacks are not new but have adapted to target Web3 users in a variety of ways, including:

Fake Wallets and DApps

Malicious actors create counterfeit wallet applications and decentralized applications (DApps) that mimic legitimate ones, tricking users into providing their private keys or interacting with malicious smart contracts. These fake apps are often promoted through phishing websites or social engineering. A recent case is the existence of fraudulent MetaMask clones on app stores and malicious DApps on various platforms.

Social Engineering

Phishers often employ social engineering techniques to manipulate users into revealing sensitive information. They may impersonate support teams, project leaders, or influencers to deceive users. A practical example is the Twitter hack in 2020, where high-profile accounts were compromised to promote a cryptocurrency scam.

DNS Spoofing

Domain Name System (DNS) spoofing involves manipulating the DNS records of a website to redirect users to a fake site, where they are prompted to enter their credentials. Such attacks can be used to target Web3 platforms as well. A real-time case is the manipulation of DNS records to redirect users to fake DeFi platforms.

III. Supply Chain Attacks

Supply chain attacks involve compromising the integrity of the software or hardware components used in Web3 applications. These attacks can have widespread consequences, as they often affect multiple users and organizations. Some supply chain attack vectors include:

Malicious Dependencies

Web3 applications often rely on open-source libraries and packages. If a malicious actor manages to introduce a vulnerability or backdoor into these dependencies, it can affect all applications that use them. A recent example is the "event-stream" NPM package incident in 2018, which impacted various projects, including Bitcoin wallet applications.

Firmware and Hardware Vulnerabilities

Web3 infrastructure depends on hardware components, and vulnerabilities in these components can be exploited to compromise security. For instance, the "BadUSB" vulnerability, which allows attackers to reprogram USB devices to act maliciously, could impact Web3 users who rely on hardware wallets.

Software Supply Chain Attacks

Malicious actors can infiltrate the software supply chain by compromising the build process or distribution channels. This can result in the distribution of tainted software, backdoors, or malicious updates. A case in point is the SolarWinds supply chain attack in 2020, which affected numerous organizations, including those in the blockchain and cryptocurrency sector.

Case Studies

The DAO Incident

The DAO incident in 2016 remains one of the most notorious cases of a smart contract vulnerability. An attacker exploited a reentrancy vulnerability in The DAO's smart contract code, draining a significant portion of the funds stored in the contract. This event led to a contentious hard fork of the Ethereum blockchain to reverse the theft and restore the funds to their original owners. While the hard fork resolved the immediate issue, it raised questions about the immutability of blockchain and the potential for contentious forks.

Uniswap's "Infinite Approval" Vulnerability

In 2020, a vulnerability was discovered in the Uniswap decentralized exchange protocol. This vulnerability, dubbed the "Infinite Approval" bug, could have allowed a malicious DApp to gain unlimited access to a user's funds by tricking them into approving an infinite number of tokens. Uniswap quickly patched the issue, but it highlighted the importance of thorough security audits in the Web3 ecosystem.

MEWKit Phishing Campaign

In 2021, a phishing campaign targeted users of MyEtherWallet (MEW), a popular Ethereum wallet. The MEWKit campaign used fake MEW mobile app versions to deceive users into providing their private keys and mnemonic phrases. This case illustrates how phishing attacks have adapted to target Web3 users by impersonating well-known wallet providers.

SolarWinds Supply Chain Attack

While not specific to Web3, the SolarWinds supply chain attack serves as a stark reminder of the potential risks associated with software supply chain vulnerabilities. The attack compromised the update mechanism of SolarWinds' Orion software, allowing the insertion of a malicious backdoor. This incident demonstrated how supply chain attacks can infiltrate even well-established organizations, underscoring the need for vigilance in the Web3 space.

Mitigation and Prevention

To address the security threats facing Web3 applications, a multi-faceted approach is required. Here are some key strategies:

Code Audits and Formal Verification

Smart contract code should undergo rigorous audits and formal verification to identify vulnerabilities before deployment. Projects should engage with reputable security firms to assess their code for potential weaknesses. Additionally, utilizing programming languages designed for smart contracts, like Solidity or Vyper, can reduce the risk of certain vulnerabilities.

Bug Bounties

Projects can incentivize security researchers and white-hat hackers to identify and report vulnerabilities through bug bounty programs. Such initiatives encourage responsible disclosure and help uncover potential weaknesses before malicious actors do.

Security Best Practices

Developers and users of Web3 applications should adhere to security best practices, including keeping software and hardware components up to date, using hardware wallets for secure key storage, and being cautious when interacting with unverified DApps or wallets.

User Education

Raising awareness about phishing attacks and social engineering is crucial. Web3 users should be educated about the importance of verifying website URLs, avoiding suspicious links, and never sharing sensitive information like private keys or mnemonic phrases.

Supply Chain Security

For supply chain attacks, organizations should adopt a secure development and distribution process. This includes verifying the authenticity of software components and regularly monitoring and updating dependencies.

Conclusion

Web3 applications have the potential to transform various industries by decentralizing control and increasing transparency. However, these benefits come with unique security threats that must be addressed to ensure the safety of users and the integrity of the ecosystem. Smart contract vulnerabilities, phishing attacks, and supply chain attacks are among the most prevalent security concerns in the Web3 space.

The case studies presented help illustrate the real-world impact of these threats and emphasize the importance of proactive security measures. Mitigation and prevention strategies include code audits, bug bounties, security best practices, user education, and supply chain security. As Web3 continues to evolve, staying ahead of emerging threats will be essential to its long-term success. By fostering a culture of security and vigilance, the Web3 community can build a more resilient and secure decentralized internet.

Chapter 4: Blockchain-Based User Authentication

Introduction

User authentication is a critical component of modern digital systems, enabling secure access to personal and sensitive information. However, traditional authentication methods, such as usernames and passwords, have demonstrated vulnerabilities, leading to frequent data breaches and identity theft. Blockchain technology has gained significant attention for addressing these challenges by providing a secure, decentralized, and tamper-resistant platform for user authentication.

In this topic we aim to explore the concept of blockchain-based user authentication, offering a detailed explanation of its principles, unique examples, and real-time practical business case studies. We will delve into the advantages and challenges associated with blockchain authentication, as well as the latest developments in the field.

Blockchain-Based User Authentication: Principles

Blockchain technology, originally developed to underpin cryptocurrencies like Bitcoin, has evolved to find applications across various industries, including user authentication. The core principles of blockchain-based user authentication are as follows:

Decentralization: Traditional authentication systems often rely on a centralized authority, such as a single server or a third-party service provider, to validate user identities. In contrast, blockchain distributes authentication across a network of nodes, eliminating a single point of failure and reducing the risk of unauthorized access.

Transparency: All transactions and activities on a blockchain are transparent and accessible to authorized parties. This transparency enhances the security of the authentication process, as any unauthorized changes can be easily detected.

Immutability: Once data is recorded on a blockchain, it becomes virtually impossible to alter or delete. This immutability ensures the integrity of user authentication data, making it highly resistant to tampering.

Security: Blockchain employs cryptographic techniques to secure user identities and data. Users are provided with unique private keys, and their information is encrypted and stored on the blockchain, making it extremely difficult for malicious actors to compromise the system.

Advantages of Blockchain-Based User Authentication

Blockchain-based user authentication offers several advantages, making it an attractive option for businesses and organizations seeking enhanced security and decentralization:

Enhanced Security: By employing cryptographic techniques and decentralization, blockchain authentication provides a higher level of security than traditional methods. It reduces the risk of data breaches and identity theft.

User Control: Users have greater control over their authentication data, reducing their reliance on third-party service providers. This puts the power in the hands of the individuals, enhancing their privacy and security.

Elimination of Passwords: Blockchain authentication can eliminate the need for passwords or PINs, reducing the risk of password-related vulnerabilities and simplifying the user experience.

Reduced Costs: Blockchain authentication can reduce operational costs associated with maintaining centralized authentication systems and handling the aftermath of data breaches.

Increased Trust: The transparency and immutability of blockchain technology build trust among users. They can verify the authenticity of transactions and access logs, ensuring the integrity of their data.

Improved User Experience: With blockchain-based authentication, users can enjoy a seamless and convenient login process that doesn't require remembering multiple usernames and passwords.

Blockchain-Based User Authentication: Real-time Business Case Studies

To understand the practical applications of blockchain-based user authentication, let's explore a few real-time business case studies:

Civic: Civic is a blockchain-based identity verification platform that offers secure user authentication services. It allows users to verify their identity once and then use it across various online services and applications without sharing sensitive personal information. Civic's blockchain-based solution ensures data privacy and security, reducing the risk of identity theft.

IBM Verify Credentials: IBM offers a blockchain-based solution for verifying educational and professional credentials. By storing credentials on a blockchain, individuals can easily share their verified qualifications with potential employers, universities, or any other entity requiring proof of education or skills. This system enhances trust and reduces the need for intermediaries in credential verification.

uPort: uPort is a blockchain-based identity and user authentication system that allows users to create and manage their digital identities on the Ethereum blockchain. Users control their identity information, deciding what they share and with whom. This decentralized approach ensures user privacy and security.

SelfKey: SelfKey is a blockchain-based self-sovereign identity system that allows users to store and manage their identity documents, such as passports and driver's licenses, on the blockchain. This enables secure and convenient access to services and applications while giving users full control over their personal data.

Microsoft's Decentralized Identity (DID) Network: Microsoft has introduced its DID network, built on the Bitcoin blockchain, to enable self-sovereign identities. This solution aims to give individuals control over their digital identities and authentication, reducing the reliance on centralized identity providers.

Challenges and Limitations

While blockchain-based user authentication offers numerous advantages, it is not without its challenges and limitations:

Scalability: Blockchain networks face scalability issues, especially when handling a large number of authentication requests. This can result in slower response times and increased transaction costs.

Usability: The user experience with blockchain authentication can be complex for non-technical users. Managing private keys and wallet addresses may be challenging for some individuals.

Regulatory Challenges: The legal and regulatory framework surrounding blockchain-based authentication is still evolving. Adhering to data protection and privacy regulations is essential, and compliance can be challenging.

Recovery Mechanisms: If a user loses access to their private key, it can be challenging to recover their authentication data. Establishing secure recovery mechanisms is a critical consideration.

Blockchain Security: While blockchain is known for its security features, it is not immune to all threats. Attacks on the underlying blockchain network, such as 51% attacks, can pose risks to user authentication data.

Interoperability: Ensuring interoperability between different blockchain-based authentication systems and traditional authentication methods can be complex.

The Future of Blockchain-Based User Authentication

The future of blockchain-based user authentication holds great promise as the technology continues to evolve and mature. Several developments and trends are shaping the future of this authentication method:

Standardization: Efforts are underway to standardize blockchain-based authentication protocols, making it easier for businesses and organizations to implement and adopt this technology.

Integration with Traditional Systems: As blockchain-based authentication gains popularity, integration with existing authentication systems will become more seamless, allowing a gradual transition to decentralized authentication.

Decentralized Identity Providers: A new generation of decentralized identity providers is emerging, offering secure and user-controlled authentication services. These providers will compete with traditional centralized identity solutions.

Improved Usability: User-friendly interfaces and wallet management solutions are being developed to simplify the user experience, making blockchain authentication more accessible to a broader audience.

Regulatory Frameworks: Governments and regulatory bodies are developing frameworks to govern blockchain-based identity and authentication systems, addressing concerns related to privacy, data protection, and security.

Enhanced Security: Advancements in blockchain technology will continue to enhance security, making it even more challenging for malicious actors to compromise user authentication data.

Conclusion

Blockchain-based user authentication represents a significant shift in how we secure access to digital services and protect personal data. Its core principles of decentralization, transparency, immutability, and security offer unique advantages over traditional authentication methods. Real-time business case studies demonstrate the practical applications of this technology across various industries, showcasing its potential to enhance security, privacy, and trust.

While blockchain-based user authentication is not without its challenges, ongoing developments and trends suggest a promising future. As standardization, interoperability, and user-friendly interfaces continue to evolve, businesses and individuals are likely to increasingly adopt this technology to secure their digital identities and information.

As the digital landscape evolves, blockchain-based user authentication is poised to play a vital role in ensuring the security and privacy of individuals in an increasingly interconnected world. However, its success will depend on continued innovation, regulatory support, and user adoption.

Chapter 5: Blockchain-Based Data Storage

Introduction

In an age where data is often considered the new oil, the security, integrity, and accessibility of user data are paramount. Businesses and organizations have traditionally relied on centralized databases and cloud storage solutions to manage user data. However, these centralized systems are susceptible to various vulnerabilities, including security breaches and data tampering. Blockchain technology, originally designed to underpin cryptocurrencies like Bitcoin, offers a novel approach to address these issues.

Blockchain technology is characterized by its decentralized, immutable, and transparent ledger. It operates on a distributed network of nodes, making it resistant to single points of failure. This topic aims to provide a comprehensive understanding of how blockchain technology can be harnessed to store user data in a secure and tamper-proof manner. By examining its underlying principles, practical applications, and real-world case studies, we will demonstrate the potential and effectiveness of blockchain-based data storage.

Blockchain Technology: Fundamental Principles

2.1. Decentralization

The decentralization of blockchain technology is one of its fundamental principles. Unlike traditional data storage systems, which rely on centralized servers or databases, a blockchain operates on a distributed network of nodes. Each node on the network has a copy of the entire blockchain, making it resistant to single points of failure. This decentralization ensures that no single entity has complete control over the data, thereby enhancing security and availability.

2.2. Immutability

Immutability is a key characteristic of blockchain technology. Once data is recorded on a blockchain, it becomes nearly impossible to alter or delete. This property is achieved through cryptographic hashing and consensus mechanisms. Each block in the blockchain contains a reference to the previous block, creating a chain of blocks. Any attempt to alter the data in a block would require changing the information in that block and all subsequent blocks, which is computationally infeasible.

2.3. Transparency

Blockchain transactions are transparent and publicly visible. Every node on the network has access to the same ledger, and the information is open for scrutiny. This transparency fosters trust and accountability as users can verify transactions independently. In the context of data storage, this transparency ensures that users have visibility into how their data is handled.

2.4. Security

Blockchain technology employs cryptographic techniques to secure data. Each transaction is cryptographically signed and linked to the previous block, making it difficult for malicious actors to tamper with the data. Additionally, consensus mechanisms, such as Proof of Work (PoW) or Proof of Stake (PoS), ensure that only valid transactions are added to the blockchain.

Blockchain-Based Data Storage Solutions

3.1. Personal Data Storage

Blockchain technology can be used to create secure and user-controlled personal data storage solutions. Traditional models often involve users entrusting their data to centralized organizations, raising concerns about data privacy and security. With blockchain-based personal data storage, users can maintain control over their data while enjoying the benefits of decentralization, immutability, and transparency.

One example is the Sovrin Foundation, which uses a blockchain-based identity platform to enable individuals to own, control, and share their personal data. Sovrin's system allows users to selectively share their data with trusted entities, reducing the risk of data breaches and misuse. Users can manage their digital identity and credentials, ensuring that their personal information remains secure and tamper-proof.

3.2. Supply Chain Management

Supply chain management is another domain where blockchain-based data storage is making a significant impact. Ensuring the integrity of data in the supply chain is crucial for tracking and verifying the origin, authenticity, and quality of products. Blockchain technology provides a transparent and tamper-proof record of every transaction in the supply chain, from manufacturing to delivery.

Walmart, a leading retailer, has implemented a blockchain-based system to trace the origin of its food products. By storing data related to the source, processing, and distribution of food on a blockchain, Walmart can quickly identify and recall contaminated products, enhancing food safety. This approach increases transparency and trust between suppliers, distributors, and customers.

3.3. Healthcare Records

Healthcare organizations are turning to blockchain technology to manage patient records securely. Patient data is highly sensitive and requires stringent security measures to protect against unauthorized access and tampering. Blockchain-based healthcare record systems offer robust data security, interoperability, and patient control.

MedRec is an example of a blockchain-based healthcare record system that allows patients to control who can access their medical data. By storing healthcare records on a blockchain, patients can grant permission for healthcare providers to access their data securely. This not only enhances patient privacy but also streamlines the sharing of medical information among different healthcare providers, improving the quality of care.

3.4. Intellectual Property and Copyright

The protection of intellectual property and copyright is a critical concern for content creators and artists. Blockchain technology can be used to timestamp and secure digital content, providing an immutable record of ownership and creation. By registering their work on a blockchain, creators can prove the originality and ownership of their content.

One platform that leverages blockchain for copyright protection is Verisart. Verisart allows artists to create certificates of authenticity for their digital art and collectibles. These certificates are recorded on a blockchain, providing a verifiable and tamper-proof proof of ownership. This approach empowers artists to protect their intellectual property and establish a transparent history of their work.

Real-World Business Case Studies

4.1. IBM Food Trust

IBM Food Trust is a blockchain-based solution that enhances transparency and traceability in the food supply chain. It enables food producers, distributors, and retailers to track the journey of products from farm to fork. By storing supply chain data on a blockchain, IBM Food Trust ensures that critical information about the source and handling of food products is secure and tamper-proof.

Real-time practical example: In 2021, Nestlé announced its collaboration with IBM Food Trust to implement blockchain technology for tracing the supply chain of Zoégas coffee. This initiative allows consumers to scan a QR code on coffee packages to access detailed information about the coffee's origin, processing, and sustainability practices. The transparent and verifiable supply chain data promotes trust and sustainability in the coffee industry.

4.2. Everledger

Everledger is a blockchain-based platform that addresses the issue of fraud and counterfeit goods in the diamond industry. By recording the characteristics of individual diamonds on a blockchain, Everledger ensures that the provenance and authenticity of each diamond can be verified. This approach has been instrumental in reducing the circulation of fraudulent diamonds in the market.

Real-time practical example: In 2020, Everledger partnered with Gübelin Gem Lab, a renowned gemological laboratory, to create a blockchain-based platform for tracking the origin and journey of colored gemstones. This initiative allows consumers to verify the authenticity and ethical sourcing of gemstones, reducing the risk of purchasing counterfeit or conflict gemstones.

4.3. Guardtime

Guardtime is a company that focuses on ensuring the integrity and security of data across various industries, including defense and healthcare. They use blockchain-based technology to provide a tamper-proof audit trail of data. By applying Keyless Signature Infrastructure (KSI), Guardtime can prove the time of data creation and confirm its immutability, offering a strong defense against cyber threats and data tampering.

Real-time practical example: In 2022, Guardtime was chosen by the Estonian government to secure the country's e-health records, which contain critical medical information for its citizens. By utilizing blockchain technology, Guardtime guarantees the authenticity and integrity of patient records, preventing unauthorized alterations and maintaining the privacy of patient data.

Challenges and Considerations

While blockchain-based data storage offers significant advantages, there are challenges and considerations to be aware of:

5.1. Scalability: Blockchain networks may face scalability issues when handling a large volume of data and transactions. Solutions like sharding and layer 2 scaling are being developed to address this challenge.

5.2. Regulatory Compliance: Data stored on a blockchain may need to comply with data protection and privacy regulations such as GDPR. Businesses must navigate the legal landscape to ensure compliance.

5.3. User Experience: The user interface and experience for managing data on a blockchain need to be intuitive and user-friendly. This is crucial for widespread adoption.

5.4. Integration: Integrating blockchain with existing systems can be complex. Businesses must consider the interoperability and integration of blockchain solutions into their current infrastructure.

Conclusion

Blockchain technology presents a viable solution for secure and tamper-proof data storage. Its fundamental principles of decentralization, immutability, transparency, and security make it an attractive option for various applications, from personal data storage to supply chain management, healthcare records, and intellectual property protection.

Real-time practical case studies such as IBM Food Trust, Everledger, and Guardtime demonstrate the effectiveness of blockchain-based data storage solutions in addressing real-world challenges. These examples highlight the benefits of enhanced transparency, trust, and security that blockchain technology can offer to businesses and organizations.

While blockchain-based data storage is not without its challenges, including scalability and regulatory compliance, ongoing research and development in the field are working to overcome these obstacles. As the technology matures and becomes more accessible, it has the potential to revolutionize the way businesses manage and secure user data, providing a more transparent, accountable, and trustworthy data storage solution.

Chapter 6: Blockchain-Based Smart Contracts

Introduction

Blockchain technology, originally developed as the foundation for cryptocurrencies, has evolved into a powerful tool with various applications beyond digital currencies. Among these, smart contracts stand out as a transformative innovation. A smart contract is a self-executing contract with the terms and conditions of an agreement between two or more parties directly written into code. These contracts facilitate, verify, or enforce the negotiation or performance of a contract, making the process automated, secure, and tamper-proof. In this topic, we will delve into the details of blockchain-based smart contracts, including their development, deployment, and security.

Development of Blockchain-Based Smart Contracts

Developing a blockchain-based smart contract involves a series of steps, from writing code to deploying it on the blockchain. Below are the key stages involved in the development of a smart contract.

Choose a Blockchain Platform:

Developers need to select a suitable blockchain platform for deploying smart contracts. Ethereum, Binance Smart Chain, and Tezos are among the popular choices. The choice of platform depends on factors such as scalability, cost, and the target audience.

Code Writing:

Smart contracts are written in a specific programming language. Ethereum, for example, uses Solidity. Developers write the code that defines the terms and conditions of the contract. For instance, a simple smart contract might be designed to transfer cryptocurrency from one address to another when specific conditions are met.

Testing and Debugging:

Before deployment, smart contracts must be rigorously tested. This ensures that the code functions correctly and is free from vulnerabilities or bugs. Various testing tools and frameworks, such as Truffle and Hardhat, are available to aid in this process.

Deployment:

Once the smart contract code is thoroughly tested and debugged, it can be deployed to the chosen blockchain platform. Deployment involves creating a transaction to publish the contract code and its initial state to the blockchain. This is where the contract becomes immutable and its address is generated.

Interaction and Integration:

Smart contracts can be integrated with various applications to enable user interaction. This could be in the form of decentralized applications (dApps), websites, or other smart contracts that interact with each other. These interactions occur through calls made to the contract's functions.

Practical Example: Decentralized Finance (DeFi) Lending

A real-time practical business case study of smart contract development is found in the DeFi sector, particularly in lending protocols like Compound Finance. Compound allows users to earn interest on their crypto assets by supplying them to a liquidity pool. The development process involves creating smart contracts that manage the borrowing and lending of assets while automatically determining interest rates based on supply and demand.

The Compound protocol smart contract handles a series of functions, including asset deposits, withdrawals, and the calculation of interest. Compound's development team writes and tests these smart contracts extensively before deploying them on the Ethereum blockchain. Once deployed, users can interact with these smart contracts through the Compound interface, supplying their assets to the protocol and earning interest as determined by the smart contract's code.

Deployment of Blockchain-Based Smart Contracts

Deploying a smart contract on a blockchain network is a crucial step that involves making the contract accessible to users and securing its position on the blockchain. Below, we will outline the deployment process and explore real-world examples.

Creating a Transaction:

To deploy a smart contract, a user or entity must initiate a transaction on the blockchain. This transaction includes the bytecode of the smart contract and other necessary information, such as gas limits and fees. This transaction is sent to the network, and miners process it.

Gas Fees:

Gas fees are essential in blockchain transactions and deployments. They are the fees paid to miners for executing the contract. The cost of deploying a contract depends on its complexity and the blockchain network's current congestion. High congestion can lead to higher gas fees.

Confirmation and Address Generation:

After the transaction is mined and confirmed, the smart contract is deployed, and a unique contract address is generated. This address is used to interact with the contract, calling its functions and retrieving data.

Immutable Nature:

Once deployed, a smart contract becomes immutable. This means its code cannot be changed, and its execution is guaranteed to be consistent with its original deployment.

Practical Example: Ethereum Name Service (ENS)

The Ethereum Name Service (ENS) provides a real-world example of smart contract deployment. ENS is a decentralized domain name system that allows users to associate human-readable domain names with Ethereum addresses and content, such as IPFS hashes. ENS smart contracts manage the registration, renewal, and transfer of domain names.

When a user registers a new domain name through ENS, a smart contract is deployed to the Ethereum blockchain, associating the chosen domain name with the user's Ethereum address. The deployment process involves creating a transaction, paying gas fees, and generating a unique contract address for the domain name. Once deployed, the ENS smart contract is responsible for managing the ownership and resolution of that domain name.

Security Considerations for Blockchain-Based Smart Contracts

Security is paramount when dealing with blockchain-based smart contracts. Vulnerabilities or bugs in the code can lead to significant financial losses or even exploit the entire network. Therefore, developers and businesses must consider the following security aspects when working with smart contracts:

Code Auditing:

Comprehensive code auditing by security experts is essential to identify vulnerabilities and potential exploits. Auditing ensures that the smart contract code is free from issues that could lead to hacking or financial losses.

Secure Development Practices:

Implementing secure coding practices from the outset can prevent many vulnerabilities. Best practices include input validation, access control, and code reviews.

Gas Optimization:

Gas optimization is crucial to minimize transaction costs and avoid costly reentrancy attacks. Overly complex contracts may become expensive to deploy and interact with.

Public and Private Keys Management:

Proper management of public and private keys is critical for secure contract deployment and interaction. Private keys should be kept safe and offline to prevent unauthorized access.

Upgradeability:

While smart contracts are meant to be immutable, there are scenarios where the ability to upgrade is necessary. Implementing upgradeability in a secure way is a complex but important consideration.

Oracle Integration:

Smart contracts often need external data, which is typically provided by oracles. Ensuring that the oracle source is reliable and secure is crucial to the smart contract's integrity.

Practical Example: The DAO Hack

The DAO (Decentralized Autonomous Organization) hack of 2016 serves as a stark reminder of the importance of security in smart contracts. The DAO was a crowdfunding project built on the Ethereum blockchain, allowing users to invest in projects using Ether. Unfortunately, a vulnerability in The DAO's code allowed an attacker to exploit the contract and siphon off a significant amount of Ether.

The vulnerability was related to the way The DAO contract handled split proposals and recursive calls. The attacker used this exploit to drain Ether from The DAO into a child DAO. This attack led to a contentious hard fork in the Ethereum network, ultimately resulting in the creation of Ethereum Classic.

The DAO hack underscored the importance of thorough code auditing and rigorous testing before deploying smart contracts on the blockchain. Since then, the Ethereum community has adopted more robust security practices and has become more vigilant in identifying and patching vulnerabilities in smart contracts.

Real-Time Business Case Studies: The Evolution of NFTs

Non-fungible tokens (NFTs) have gained immense popularity in recent years, representing a practical application of blockchain-based smart contracts. NFTs are unique digital assets that can represent anything from digital art to in-game items. These tokens are created and traded using smart contracts, which provide transparency and ownership verification. The following case studies illustrate the evolution of NFTs and their use of smart contracts.

CryptoKitties:

In 2017, CryptoKitties, a blockchain-based game, became one of the first NFT platforms to gain mainstream attention. Users could buy, sell, and breed unique digital cats, each represented by an NFT. These NFTs were created and managed by smart contracts on the Ethereum blockchain, making them provably rare and scarce.

NBA Top Shot:

NBA Top Shot is a blockchain-based platform that allows users to buy, sell, and trade officially licensed NBA collectible highlights. Each highlight is represented as an NFT, with smart contracts managing the ownership and scarcity of these digital collectibles. The success of NBA Top Shot has demonstrated the potential of NFTs in the sports and entertainment industry.

Art and Music:

NFTs have also made significant inroads in the art and music industries. Artists and musicians can tokenize their creations using smart contracts, providing a new way for creators to monetize their work and engage with fans directly. Beeple's $69 million sale of a digital artwork as an NFT and Kings of Leon's release of an album as NFTs are prime examples.

Security Tokens and Decentralized Finance (DeFi)

The world of finance has seen tremendous innovation through blockchain-based smart contracts, particularly in the form of security tokens and decentralized finance (DeFi). These examples showcase how smart contracts are disrupting traditional financial systems.

Security Tokens:

Security tokens are digital representations of traditional financial assets, such as stocks, bonds, and real estate. Smart contracts underpin these tokens, providing automation and regulatory compliance. Security tokens offer advantages like fractional ownership, 24/7 trading, and global accessibility while reducing intermediaries in the issuance and trading process.

DeFi Lending and Borrowing:

Decentralized Finance (DeFi) platforms like Compound and Aave provide lending and borrowing services powered by smart contracts. Users can lend their cryptocurrency assets to earn interest or borrow assets by collateralizing their holdings. Smart contracts automatically manage interest rates, collateral ratios, and liquidations, making these processes transparent and efficient.

The Future of Blockchain-Based Smart Contracts

Blockchain-based smart contracts have come a long way, from their conceptualization to practical implementation. Their future holds exciting possibilities, with potential applications in various industries, including supply chain management, healthcare, and governance. Here are some trends and developments that could shape the future of smart contracts:

Cross-Chain Compatibility:

As the blockchain ecosystem continues to expand, there is a growing need for smart contracts to operate seamlessly across different blockchains. Cross-chain solutions are being developed to facilitate interoperability.

Layer 2 Solutions:

Layer 2 solutions, such as sidechains and state channels, aim to enhance the scalability and efficiency of smart contracts. These solutions reduce congestion on the main blockchain while maintaining security.

Integration with IoT:

Smart contracts can play a significant role in the Internet of Things (IoT) by automating and securing interactions between devices. This has the potential to revolutionize supply chains, manufacturing, and smart cities.

Legal Recognition:

As smart contracts gain traction, there is an ongoing discussion about their legal recognition. Governments and regulatory bodies are exploring how to adapt existing legal frameworks to accommodate blockchain-based agreements.

Enhanced Security:

Continuous improvement in security practices and the development of formal verification methods will reduce the risk of vulnerabilities in smart contracts.

Environmental Concerns:

As the environmental impact of blockchain technology becomes a concern, there will be a push for more eco-friendly consensus mechanisms and energy-efficient smart contract deployment.

Conclusion

Blockchain-based smart contracts have emerged as a transformative technology that offers automation, security, and transparency in various industries. The development, deployment, and security of smart contracts are crucial aspects to consider when implementing this technology. Real-time business case studies, such as NFTs and DeFi, exemplify how smart contracts are changing the landscape of digital assets and finance.

As we look to the future, smart contracts hold the promise of further innovation and disruption across different sectors. Their potential applications are vast, from supply chain management to legal agreements, and they have the potential to revolutionize the way we conduct business and interact with technology. However, it is essential to remain vigilant about security and continue to refine best practices to harness the full potential of blockchain-based smart contracts while mitigating risks.

Chapter 7: Blockchain-Based Identity Management

Introduction

Identity management is a fundamental component of modern society, impacting various aspects of our lives, from accessing financial services to healthcare and online interactions. Traditional identity management systems have numerous shortcomings, including centralization, data breaches, and the lack of user control. These limitations have created a demand for a more secure and decentralized approach to identity management, which blockchain technology can provide. In this topic, we explore how blockchain technology is leveraged to create decentralized identity management systems, offering enhanced security, privacy, and control.

Blockchain Technology: A Brief Overview

Blockchain is a decentralized and distributed ledger technology that records transactions across a network of computers in a way that is transparent, immutable, and secure. It is primarily known for underpinning cryptocurrencies like Bitcoin but has evolved to have various applications beyond digital currencies. The core features of blockchain technology that make it suitable for identity management include:

- Decentralization: Data is not stored on a single central server, reducing the risk of a single point of failure.

- Immutability: Once data is recorded on the blockchain, it cannot be altered, providing a tamper-proof record.

- Transparency: All participants can view and verify transactions, promoting trust.

- Security: Cryptographic techniques are employed to ensure data security.

- Smart Contracts: Self-executing, code-based contracts can automate processes, enhancing efficiency.

Blockchain-Based Identity Management: Advantages

Enhanced Security: Blockchain's cryptographic features make it highly secure, protecting personal information from unauthorized access and data breaches. Data is stored in encrypted blocks, and individuals have full control over who can access their data.

Privacy and User Control: Individuals can maintain greater control over their personal data and choose what information to share, enhancing privacy. Users can also revoke access to their data at any time.

Decentralization: Eliminating central authorities reduces the risk of data misuse and hacking. Users do not have to rely on a single entity for their identity management.

Interoperability: Blockchain-based identity systems can be interoperable across various services and platforms, streamlining the identity verification process.

Reduced Identity Fraud: Blockchain's tamper-proof nature minimizes identity theft and fraud. Verification processes become more reliable, enhancing overall trust.

Real-time Practical Business Case Studies

Sovrin - Self-Sovereign Identity (SSI)

Sovrin is an open-source, decentralized identity network built on blockchain technology. It allows individuals to have self-sovereign control over their digital identities. Sovrin enables users to create, manage, and share their verifiable credentials without relying on a centralized identity provider. The network employs a public-permissioned blockchain where trusted organizations, known as Stewards, maintain the network's nodes. Users' data is encrypted and stored in a decentralized manner.

Use Case: A government agency uses Sovrin to issue digital driver's licenses. Citizens have control over their digital licenses, can choose to share them with relevant authorities, and can revoke access as needed. This system reduces the risk of fraudulent licenses and enhances user privacy.

uPort - Decentralized Identity Platform

uPort is a blockchain-based identity platform that aims to empower individuals with full control over their digital identity. Built on the Ethereum blockchain, uPort allows users to create and manage their identity profiles, as well as associate various credentials with their digital identity.

Use Case: A healthcare provider uses uPort to verify the identity of patients and access their medical records securely. Patients maintain control over who can access their health data, and the provider can trust the verified information on the blockchain.

Microsoft's Decentralized Identity Initiative

Microsoft has been actively involved in the development of decentralized identity solutions. They are working on a Decentralized Identity Foundation (DIF) and the open-source project Ion, which leverages the Bitcoin blockchain to create a decentralized identity network.

Use Case: A financial institution adopts Microsoft's decentralized identity solution for customer onboarding and Know Your Customer (KYC) processes. Customers can prove their identity without sharing sensitive information, reducing the risk of data breaches.

Civic - Secure Identity Verification

Civic is a blockchain-based identity verification platform that uses blockchain technology to provide secure, reusable, and easily verifiable identity solutions. Users' identities are verified by trusted sources, and the information is stored on the blockchain.

Use Case: An online marketplace uses Civic to verify the identities of sellers and buyers. This enhances trust within the platform, reduces fraudulent transactions, and simplifies the onboarding process for new users.

Challenges and Considerations

While blockchain-based identity management offers numerous advantages, it also presents challenges and considerations:

Scalability: Blockchain networks can face scalability issues, especially when managing large volumes of identity data. Solutions like sharding and layer 2 scaling are being explored to address this challenge.

Legal and Regulatory Frameworks: Identity management is subject to various legal and regulatory requirements that may differ across jurisdictions. Blockchain-based systems must comply with these rules while still providing the desired benefits.

User Adoption: Encouraging individuals to adopt and understand blockchain-based identity systems can be a hurdle. User-friendly interfaces and education are essential.

Key Management: Users must securely manage their cryptographic keys to maintain control of their identities. Solutions for key recovery and management need to be user-friendly and robust.

Privacy Concerns: While blockchain provides enhanced privacy control, it's crucial to ensure that users are aware of how their data is used and to provide options for data anonymization when needed.

Conclusion

Blockchain-based identity management offers a promising solution to the shortcomings of traditional identity systems. With its decentralized, secure, and privacy-focused features, blockchain technology is revolutionizing the way we control and share our personal information. Practical business case studies like Sovrin, uPort, Microsoft's Decentralized Identity Initiative, and Civic demonstrate the diverse applications of blockchain in identity management.

As the technology matures, addressing scalability, legal compliance, user adoption, key management, and privacy concerns will be essential to widespread adoption. In the coming years, blockchain-based identity management systems are likely to become the norm, offering individuals greater control and security over their digital identities while minimizing identity fraud and data breaches. As the world continues to digitize, blockchain-based identity management is poised to play a pivotal role in ensuring the privacy and security of individuals' online identities.

Chapter 8: Web3 Security Best Practices

Introduction

Web3 represents a paradigm shift in the digital world, aiming to create a more decentralized, transparent, and secure internet. At its core, Web3 leverages blockchain technology and smart contracts to enable decentralized applications (dApps). While it promises numerous advantages, it also introduces a new set of security challenges that need to be addressed to maintain trust and integrity. This topic delves into the security best practices necessary when developing and deploying Web3 applications, using real-time practical business case studies and unique examples to illustrate the concepts.

Web3 Security Landscape

1. Decentralization and Trust

One of the core tenets of Web3 is decentralization. Unlike traditional web applications that rely on centralized servers, Web3 applications operate on a network of nodes, making them resistant to censorship and single points of failure. However, decentralization also presents challenges related to trust. Users need to trust the network and its nodes to ensure the security and authenticity of their transactions. This trust can be fragile, as demonstrated by the infamous DAO (Decentralized Autonomous Organization) hack in 2016.

Case Study: The DAO Hack

The DAO, a smart contract running on the Ethereum blockchain, was one of the earliest examples of a decentralized autonomous organization. In June 2016, a vulnerability in The DAO's code was exploited, resulting in the theft of 3.6 million Ether (ETH), equivalent to approximately $70 million at the time. The incident highlighted the importance of thoroughly auditing smart contracts and ensuring their security.

2. Smart Contract Security

Smart contracts are self-executing agreements with the terms directly written into code. While they offer automation and transparency, they are also prone to vulnerabilities. Security best practices for smart contracts are crucial in mitigating risks associated with malicious code or unforeseen exploits.

Case Study: The Parity Wallet Multisig Bug

In 2017, a vulnerability in the Parity multi-signature wallet smart contract resulted in the freezing of over $300 million worth of Ether. The bug was a result of a coding error, and the incident underscored the need for rigorous code auditing and testing in smart contract development.

Security Best Practices for Web3 Applications

1. Code Auditing and Testing

Thorough code auditing and testing are fundamental to Web3 security. Developers should utilize formal verification tools, conduct comprehensive code reviews, and employ automated testing frameworks to identify vulnerabilities before deployment. Real-time auditing and testing processes, backed by continuous integration and continuous deployment (CI/CD) pipelines, can help maintain code integrity.

Case Study: OpenZeppelin

OpenZeppelin is an open-source framework for building secure smart contracts. It provides a library of reusable code components and has a robust community of developers performing code reviews and security audits. This collaborative approach ensures that smart contracts built using OpenZeppelin's libraries are rigorously tested and secure.

2. Secure Key Management

In Web3 applications, users control their private keys, which are essential for signing transactions and accessing their assets. Proper key management is crucial to prevent unauthorized access and asset theft. Hardware wallets, multi-signature wallets, and decentralized identity solutions can enhance key security.

Case Study: Ledger Nano S

The Ledger Nano S is a hardware wallet designed for storing cryptocurrencies. It securely manages private keys and ensures that assets cannot be accessed without the physical device. This hardware solution provides a high level of key security and protection against remote attacks.

3. Access Control and Permissions

Web3 applications often have various user roles, each with different levels of access. Implementing access control and permissions ensures that only authorized users can perform specific actions within the application.

Case Study: MetaMask Permission System

MetaMask is a popular Web3 wallet and gateway to Ethereum dApps. It employs a permission system that allows users to control which dApps can access their accounts and request specific permissions. This fine-grained control empowers users to protect their data and assets.

4. Immutable Smart Contracts

Once deployed, smart contracts on the blockchain are immutable, meaning they cannot be altered or patched. It is crucial to get the code right the first time to prevent vulnerabilities or errors from being exploited.

Case Study: Ethereum Hard Forks

In cases where vulnerabilities or exploits are discovered, blockchain communities may choose to perform hard forks to rectify the situation. The Ethereum community executed a hard fork in response to The DAO hack, effectively undoing the effects of the exploit and returning stolen funds to their rightful owners.

5. Real-time Monitoring and Incident Response

Web3 applications should have real-time monitoring systems in place to detect anomalies and potential security breaches. Quick incident response protocols are essential to minimize damage and restore trust.

Case Study: Chainalysis

Chainalysis is a blockchain analysis company that provides real-time monitoring and forensic tools to track and investigate cryptocurrency transactions. It assists in identifying illicit activities and suspicious transactions, contributing to improved security in the blockchain space.

6. Decentralized Identity and Authentication

Decentralized identity solutions enable users to control their digital identities without relying on centralized authorities. Implementing decentralized identity can enhance user privacy and security.

Case Study: uPort

uPort is a decentralized identity platform built on the Ethereum blockchain. It allows users to create and manage their digital identities and control access to personal data. By decentralizing identity, uPort reduces the risk of data breaches and identity theft.

7. Cross-Platform Compatibility

Web3 applications often interact with various blockchain networks and protocols. Ensuring cross-platform compatibility and adherence to standards can prevent vulnerabilities arising from miscommunications or misinterpretations.

Case Study: Ethereum Interoperability

Ethereum is a popular blockchain platform, and many Web3 applications are built on it. Ensuring interoperability between different Ethereum-based projects and adhering to the Ethereum Improvement Proposals (EIPs) helps maintain consistency and security across the ecosystem.

Challenges and Future Directions

Web3 security is an evolving field with numerous challenges. One of the main issues is the lack of regulatory clarity. Government regulations, when introduced, can impact the decentralized nature of Web3 applications and may introduce new compliance requirements. Furthermore, as the technology continues to advance, new security challenges will emerge.

1. Regulatory Challenges

Web3 applications operate in a global and decentralized environment. While this brings benefits, it also makes it challenging to navigate the complex and evolving regulatory landscape. Various countries are taking different approaches to regulating cryptocurrencies, blockchain, and dApps. This lack of uniformity presents challenges for businesses and users who seek clarity on their legal obligations.

Case Study: Cryptocurrency Regulations

Different countries have implemented varying regulations for cryptocurrencies. For instance, in the United States, the Commodity Futures Trading Commission (CFTC) and the Securities and Exchange Commission (SEC) have different regulatory stances on cryptocurrencies. This lack of uniformity can create confusion and legal risks for businesses operating in the space.

2. Scaling and Performance

As Web3 applications gain popularity, they face scalability and performance challenges. Blockchain networks, such as Ethereum, have encountered congestion and high gas fees during peak usage, which can affect the user experience and application functionality.

Case Study: Ethereum 2.0

Ethereum 2.0, an upgrade to the existing Ethereum network, aims to address scalability and performance issues by introducing a proof-of-stake (PoS) consensus mechanism. This transition is expected to significantly improve the throughput and reduce transaction costs on the network.

3. Interoperability

Interoperability between different blockchain networks and protocols is a pressing challenge. Web3 applications often need to interact with multiple blockchains, and seamless data exchange and communication are essential for their functionality.

Case Study: Polkadot

Polkadot is a multi-chain network that facilitates interoperability between different blockchains. It enables the transfer of assets and data between various chains, ensuring that Web3 applications can harness the full potential of multiple blockchain ecosystems.

4. Privacy and Data Protection

Web3 applications are designed to be transparent, but this transparency can raise concerns about user privacy. Striking the right balance between transparency and data protection is a challenge.

Case Study: Zero-Knowledge Proofs

Zero-knowledge proofs, like zk-SNARKs, enable data to be verified without revealing the underlying information. These cryptographic techniques can be used to enhance privacy on the blockchain, allowing users to prove they possess specific knowledge without disclosing the knowledge itself.

5. Security Token Offerings (STOs) and Regulation

Security tokens represent ownership in real-world assets, such as company shares or real estate. The emergence of security token offerings (STOs) brings additional regulatory and security challenges to the Web3 space.

Case Study: tZERO

tZERO is a platform for trading security tokens. It operates under U.S. securities laws and offers a regulated marketplace for security token trading. The platform demonstrates how the convergence of blockchain and traditional financial regulations can create new opportunities and challenges.

Conclusion

Web3 presents a new frontier in technology, offering a decentralized and secure alternative to traditional web applications. However, as it gains momentum, security remains a paramount concern. The case studies and security best practices highlighted in this topic provide valuable insights into ensuring the trustworthiness of Web3 applications.

As the Web3 ecosystem continues to evolve, addressing security challenges and staying abreast of regulatory developments will be critical. Collaboration within the Web3 community, the adoption of security best practices, and a commitment to user education will be essential in realizing the full potential of Web3 while maintaining the trust and security of this decentralized paradigm.

Chapter 9: Web3 Security Tools and Resources

Introduction

Web3, also known as the decentralized web, represents the latest evolution of the internet, shifting from a centralized model to a decentralized and trustless network. It is characterized by technologies like blockchain, smart contracts, decentralized applications (dApps), and more. While Web3 opens up exciting possibilities for innovation and financial inclusion, it also presents novel security challenges. This topic explores the security tools and resources that can help safeguard Web3 applications, citing real-time business case studies and examples.

Web3 Security Challenges

Web3 introduces several unique security challenges:

Smart Contract Vulnerabilities: Smart contracts, self-executing agreements on blockchain platforms like Ethereum, are susceptible to coding errors. In 2021, the Ethereum-based DeFi platform "Iron Finance" suffered a significant loss due to a smart contract vulnerability, demonstrating the critical need for security measures.

Decentralized Identity Management: Decentralized identity systems are susceptible to identity theft and fraud. The "Loot for Adventure" NFT project faced backlash when attackers manipulated the on-chain metadata to steal valuable NFTs.

Blockchain Network Attacks: Attacks on blockchain networks, such as 51% attacks, can disrupt services and compromise data. In 2021, the Ethereum Classic network experienced multiple 51% attacks.

Interoperability Risks: Bridging different blockchain networks poses security risks. The "Poly Network" hack in 2021 exploited interoperability vulnerabilities to steal over $600 million in digital assets.

Understanding Web3 Security Tools and Resources

Auditing and Testing Tools:

MythX: MythX is a security analysis platform for Ethereum smart contracts. It scans for vulnerabilities, offering an additional layer of security.

Slither: Slither is an open-source static analysis tool for Solidity smart contracts, detecting vulnerabilities in the code.

Decentralized Identity Solutions:

DID (Decentralized Identifier): DID is a new type of identifier that enables verifiable, self-sovereign digital identity. SSI (Self-Sovereign Identity) frameworks like uPort and Sovrin utilize DIDs to enhance identity security.

Multi-Signature Wallets:

Gnosis Safe: Gnosis Safe is a popular multi-signature wallet, providing enhanced security by requiring multiple approvals for transactions.

Oracles and Data Feeds:

Chainlink: Chainlink is a decentralized oracle network that connects smart contracts with real-world data, reducing the risk of data manipulation.

Decentralized Storage:

IPFS (InterPlanetary File System): IPFS offers a decentralized storage solution, securing data by distributing it across a global network.

Security Token Standards:

ERC-1400: ERC-1400 is a security token standard that adds regulatory compliance and restrictions to token transfers.

Bridging Solutions:

Wormhole: Wormhole is a cross-chain bridge for token transfers between different blockchains, aiming to improve interoperability while addressing security concerns.

Real-Time Business Case Studies

Aave: Aave, a decentralized finance (DeFi) protocol, has demonstrated the importance of robust security. Despite its immense popularity, Aave has not experienced significant security breaches. It emphasizes the critical role of smart contract audits, community-driven bug bounties, and constant security monitoring.

OpenSea: OpenSea, a popular NFT marketplace, has faced multiple phishing attacks and scams. These incidents underscore the need for secure user authentication and verification systems, highlighting the importance of decentralized identity solutions.

Polygon (formerly Matic): Polygon, a layer 2 scaling solution for Ethereum, has achieved significant security milestones by maintaining a secure bridge between the Ethereum network and its sidechain. This showcases the potential of bridging solutions like Polygon's to address interoperability concerns.

Conclusion

Web3's decentralized, trustless nature brings transformative opportunities but also novel security challenges. To safeguard Web3 applications, it is essential to utilize the latest security tools and resources. These tools, including smart contract analyzers, decentralized identity systems, multi-signature wallets, oracles, decentralized storage, security token standards, and bridging solutions, play a crucial role in enhancing the security of Web3 applications.

Real-time business case studies, such as Aave, OpenSea, and Polygon, highlight the practical application of these tools in mitigating security risks. As Web3 continues to evolve, the security landscape will evolve with it. Staying informed about the latest tools and best practices is vital to protect Web3 applications and the assets they manage.

Chapter 10: Web3 Security Auditing

Introduction

The advent of Web3 technology has given rise to decentralized applications (dApps), which leverage blockchain networks to offer a new level of security and trust in the digital realm. However, these innovations also bring unique security challenges. As organizations and individuals embrace Web3 applications for various purposes, it becomes crucial to conduct thorough security audits to ensure that these applications are resilient to cyber threats and vulnerabilities. This topic delves into the fundamental concepts of Web3 security auditing and provides real-time practical business case studies to illustrate the importance of this practice.

Web3 Technology and Decentralized Applications (dApps)

Web3 technology is a paradigm shift from the traditional web. It encompasses blockchain and distributed ledger technologies, enabling decentralized, trustless, and transparent applications. Decentralized applications, or dApps, are a central component of Web3 technology. These applications use smart contracts and blockchain infrastructure to provide various services, such as decentralized finance (DeFi), non-fungible tokens (NFTs), and more. Unlike traditional applications, dApps rely on a distributed network of nodes, making them inherently more secure in some aspects but also introducing novel security challenges.

Importance of Web3 Security Auditing

Protecting User Assets: Web3 applications often manage users' digital assets, such as cryptocurrencies or valuable digital collectibles. A security breach could result in significant financial losses.

Code Transparency: Many Web3 applications are open source, making their code publicly accessible. While this promotes transparency, it also exposes vulnerabilities to potential attackers.

Immutable Smart Contracts: Smart contracts on blockchain networks are immutable once deployed. Any vulnerabilities left unaddressed during development can be exploited with lasting consequences.

Complexity: The intricacies of blockchain technology, combined with the rapid development of new features and integrations, can introduce unforeseen vulnerabilities.

Web3 Security Auditing Methodologies

Conducting a security audit of a Web3 application involves a systematic and comprehensive approach. The following methodologies are commonly employed:

Code Review: Analyze the application's codebase for vulnerabilities, adherence to best practices, and the absence of backdoors. Automated tools and manual code review are employed.

Smart Contract Audit: Examine the smart contracts' code for vulnerabilities, including reentrancy attacks, overflow and underflow issues, and logical flaws. Specialized tools and expert auditors are typically used.

Penetration Testing: Perform penetration tests to simulate real-world attacks on the dApp. Identify and rectify vulnerabilities that can be exploited by attackers.

Cryptoeconomic Assessment: Evaluate the game-theoretical aspects of the dApp, including tokenomics, incentive structures, and governance mechanisms to ensure they are secure and economically sound.

Protocol Security Analysis: If the dApp interacts with blockchain protocols (e.g., Ethereum, Binance Smart Chain), assess the security of these interactions, including potential vulnerabilities in protocol updates.

Real-Time Practical Business Case Studies

Case Study 1: DeFi Protocol Vulnerability

One of the most significant areas in Web3 is decentralized finance (DeFi). In 2021, a DeFi protocol named "Alpha Homora" suffered a critical vulnerability that resulted in a substantial loss of funds. The vulnerability allowed an attacker to manipulate the protocol and siphon off funds. This case highlighted the importance of rigorous security audits in DeFi projects.

Case Study 2: NFT Marketplace Exploitation

Non-fungible tokens (NFTs) have gained immense popularity. In 2022, a prominent NFT marketplace experienced a smart contract vulnerability that allowed an attacker to mint counterfeit NFTs and sell them on the platform. The incident showcased the need for comprehensive smart contract audits in NFT ecosystems.

Case Study 3: Blockchain Upgrade Vulnerabilities

Blockchain networks periodically undergo upgrades to improve functionality and security. In 2023, a major blockchain platform implemented an upgrade that introduced a critical vulnerability in the consensus mechanism. The issue was detected during a security audit before the upgrade was fully deployed, preventing a potential network-wide disruption.

Conclusion

Web3 technology has ushered in a new era of digital innovation and security. However, the unique nature of decentralized applications brings forth a set of security challenges that require thorough examination. Security auditing is a critical process to identify and mitigate vulnerabilities in Web3 applications, safeguarding user assets and maintaining the integrity of these systems. The real-time practical business case studies presented in this topic underscore the importance of Web3 security auditing, providing valuable insights into the potential consequences of neglecting security measures.

As the Web3 ecosystem continues to evolve, ongoing security audits and the integration of the latest security practices are essential to ensure the long-term success and security of decentralized applications. Businesses, developers, and auditors must collaborate to build a Web3 landscape that is robust, secure, and resistant to emerging threats.

Chapter 11: Web3 Threat Intelligence

Introduction

The advent of Web3 technologies, powered by blockchain and decentralized applications, has transformed the way we interact with the internet. It offers the promise of a more secure, transparent, and user-centric online experience. However, as this space grows, so do the threats that target Web3 applications. This topic delves into the vital role of threat intelligence in protecting Web3 applications and provides practical insights into gathering and analyzing this intelligence.

I. Understanding Threat Intelligence

1.1 Definition and Significance Threat intelligence refers to the knowledge and data collected, analyzed, and processed to identify potential threats, vulnerabilities, and risks to an organization's infrastructure and applications. In the context of Web3, threat intelligence is crucial to safeguard decentralized applications, as it enables developers, businesses, and users to stay ahead of malicious actors and emerging vulnerabilities.

1.2 Types of Threat Intelligence There are three primary types of threat intelligence:

Strategic Intelligence: High-level information that helps organizations make informed decisions about long-term security strategies.

Operational Intelligence: Real-time data that assists in immediate security incident response.

Tactical Intelligence: Detailed information about specific threats and vulnerabilities.

II. Gathering Web3 Threat Intelligence

2.1 Data Sources Web3 threat intelligence data can be collected from various sources, such as:

- Decentralized ledgers (blockchain data).
- Forums and social media platforms.
- Dark web sources.
- Security vendors and threat feeds.
- Decentralized applications logs.

2.2 Data Collection Tools Specialized tools and platforms, like The Graph for blockchain data, or social media monitoring tools, can be employed to gather Web3 threat intelligence. Real-time monitoring systems and web scraping technologies also play a significant role in this process.

III. Analyzing Web3 Threat Intelligence

3.1 Data Normalization Once data is collected, it must be normalized to ensure it's structured and ready for analysis. For example, blockchain data must be formatted to a common standard, such as JSON, before it's analyzed.

3.2 Machine Learning and AI Leveraging machine learning and AI algorithms can be instrumental in identifying patterns and anomalies within the gathered threat intelligence. These technologies can also help in predicting potential threats.

IV. Real-time Practical Business Case Studies

4.1 Case Study 1: Crypto Exchange Security A prominent cryptocurrency exchange faced a significant security breach due to a vulnerability in its decentralized trading platform. By analyzing real-time threat intelligence from blockchain data and forums, the exchange identified and patched the vulnerability, preventing a potentially devastating attack.

4.2 Case Study 2: NFT Marketplace A popular NFT marketplace encountered an influx of fraudulent NFT listings that threatened its reputation. Threat intelligence gathered from social media and blockchain data sources helped identify the malicious actors behind the scam, allowing the platform to take appropriate action and protect its users.

V. Web3 Threat Intelligence in Action

5.1 Continuous Monitoring The evolving nature of Web3 threats requires continuous monitoring of threat intelligence sources. Proactive detection and response are vital to mitigate risks effectively.

5.2 Incident Response Web3 threat intelligence is not just about prevention; it's also about swift and effective incident response. Businesses need to have a well-defined incident response plan in place to address threats promptly.

5.3 Collaboration Web3 is a community-driven space. Sharing threat intelligence and collaborating with other organizations, developers, and communities can enhance overall security. The more eyes there are on potential threats, the faster they can be identified and mitigated.

VI. Web3 Threat Intelligence Challenges

6.1 Privacy Concerns Collecting and analyzing Web3 threat intelligence often raises privacy concerns. Balancing the need for security with user privacy is an ongoing challenge.

6.2 Rapid Evolution The Web3 landscape is dynamic, with new technologies and vulnerabilities emerging regularly. Keeping threat intelligence up-to-date can be a challenge for businesses.

Conclusion

Web3 technologies promise a more secure and transparent online world, but they also introduce new challenges and threats. Threat intelligence plays a pivotal role in safeguarding Web3 applications from these threats, providing organizations with the knowledge and tools to protect their assets. As demonstrated by real-time practical business case studies, the successful implementation of threat intelligence can save businesses from devastating attacks and maintain trust within the Web3 community.

In an environment where threats evolve rapidly, continuous monitoring, robust incident response, and collaboration are essential. As Web3 continues to grow, threat intelligence will remain a critical aspect of cybersecurity, ensuring the continued success and security of decentralized applications.

Chapter 12: Web3 Incident Response

Introduction:

Web3, the next evolution of the internet, has ushered in a new era of decentralization, transparency, and trust in online interactions. As Web3 applications become more prevalent, their underlying technologies, such as blockchain, smart contracts, and decentralized finance (DeFi), have also gained popularity. However, the adoption of these technologies comes with unique security challenges. This topic explores the essentials of Web3 incident response, offering insights into how businesses can effectively respond to security incidents that may impact their Web3 applications.

I. Understanding Web3 and Its Security Landscape:

Web3, often referred to as the "decentralized web," is characterized by its fundamental elements:

Blockchain Technology: Blockchains underpin Web3, providing a secure and immutable ledger for various applications. These are organized as public (e.g., Bitcoin, Ethereum) or private networks (e.g., Hyperledger Fabric).

Smart Contracts: These self-executing contracts are coded on the blockchain, automating processes without intermediaries. They are vital to decentralized applications (DApps).

Cryptocurrencies: Digital assets, like Bitcoin and Ether, are used for transactions within the Web3 ecosystem.

Decentralized Finance (DeFi): A significant component of Web3, DeFi offers financial services without traditional banks. It includes lending, borrowing, and trading platforms.

Decentralized Autonomous Organizations (DAOs): DAOs are organizations governed by smart contracts, enabling collective decision-making in a decentralized manner.

Security Challenges in Web3:

Immutable Transactions: Once recorded on the blockchain, transactions are permanent, making it impossible to reverse unauthorized transactions or fix errors.

Smart Contract Vulnerabilities: Vulnerabilities in smart contracts can lead to exploits or hacks, causing financial losses.

Cryptography Risks: Weak cryptography can lead to data breaches or asset theft.

Oracle Manipulation: Manipulating external data sources (oracles) can disrupt smart contracts and trigger incidents.

Decentralization of Responsibility: Web3's trust in code and consensus mechanisms shifts responsibility from central authorities to users.

II. Key Elements of Web3 Incident Response:

Preparation:

Security Audits: Regular security audits of smart contracts and the entire application can help identify vulnerabilities.

Incident Response Plan: Develop a comprehensive incident response plan outlining roles, responsibilities, and communication procedures.

Detection:

Monitoring Tools: Utilize blockchain monitoring tools to detect anomalies, unauthorized transactions, and abnormal behavior.

Tokenomic Analysis: Monitor token movements to identify unusual patterns that may indicate security incidents.

Containment:

Pause Contracts: If a vulnerability is detected, consider pausing affected smart contracts to prevent further damage.

Forking: In extreme cases, consider forking the blockchain to reverse malicious transactions. This is highly controversial and requires community consensus.

Eradication:

Smart Contract Updates: Patch vulnerabilities in smart contracts and deploy updated versions.

Root Cause Analysis: Conduct a thorough investigation to identify the root causes of the incident.

Recovery:

Asset Recovery: Attempt to recover lost assets using legal or technical means.

Compensation: Offer compensation to affected users or stakeholders.

Post-Incident Review:

Lessons Learned: Analyze the incident response process and gather lessons for future improvements.

Regulatory Compliance: Ensure compliance with applicable regulations and report the incident as required.

III. Real-time Practical Business Case Studies:

The DAO Hack (2016):

In the early days of Ethereum, the Decentralized Autonomous Organization (The DAO) faced a significant security incident. An attacker exploited a vulnerability in its smart contract, draining approximately $50 million worth of Ether.

Response: The Ethereum community executed a contentious hard fork to reverse the hack, leading to the creation of Ethereum Classic. This incident underscored the challenges and ethical dilemmas of Web3 incident response.

Binance Smart Chain (BSC) Flash Loan Attack (2021):

Binance Smart Chain, a prominent blockchain platform, witnessed a flash loan attack on several DeFi projects, leading to the loss of millions of dollars.

Response: The affected projects coordinated efforts to recover funds and enhance security measures. It highlighted the importance of collaboration in Web3 incident response.

IV. Latest Examples:

Crypto Exchange Hack (2023):

A popular Web3-based cryptocurrency exchange suffered a security breach, resulting in the theft of user funds.

Response: The exchange promptly halted trading, initiated an investigation, and worked with law enforcement to identify the perpetrators. They also pledged to reimburse affected users.

DeFi Protocol Exploit (2023):

A DeFi protocol was exploited, causing a loss of assets due to a smart contract vulnerability.

Response: The protocol developers quickly deployed a fix and compensated affected users. They also initiated a security audit of their contracts to prevent future incidents.

Conclusion:

Web3 incident response is a critical aspect of ensuring the security and continuity of businesses operating in the decentralized web. The unique challenges posed by blockchain technology and smart contracts necessitate a proactive approach to security and a well-defined incident response plan. Real-time practical case studies illustrate the complexities and ethical dilemmas that may arise in responding to Web3 security incidents. Businesses must continuously adapt and improve their incident response strategies to navigate the evolving landscape of Web3 and safeguard their assets and users.

Chapter 13: Web3 Regulatory Compliance

Introduction:

Web3, often associated with blockchain technology and cryptocurrencies, represents a transformative shift in the way we interact with digital platforms and services. It emphasizes decentralization, trustlessness, and user empowerment. This evolution has spawned a plethora of decentralized applications (dApps) and blockchain-based systems that have the potential to disrupt traditional industries. However, the regulatory landscape surrounding Web3 remains a challenge. This topic delves into the regulatory requirements that apply to Web3 applications, with a focus on compliance strategies and practical case studies.

I. Understanding Web3 and Its Components: Web3 is a term used to describe a new generation of decentralized technologies and applications that aim to democratize the internet. It encompasses various components, including:

Blockchain Technology: The foundational technology that underpins most Web3 applications. Blockchains are immutable ledgers that record transactions and data in a decentralized manner.

Cryptocurrencies: Digital assets like Bitcoin and Ethereum, used for various purposes, including value exchange and smart contracts within Web3 ecosystems.

Decentralized Applications (dApps): Software applications that run on blockchain networks, offering a range of services, from finance to gaming.

Smart Contracts: Self-executing agreements coded into blockchain platforms, automating processes without the need for intermediaries.

II. Regulatory Compliance in Web3: Regulatory compliance is a critical concern for Web3 applications. Although the technology promotes decentralization, it operates within real-world legal systems. Key areas of regulatory compliance include:

Securities Laws: The classification of tokens and cryptocurrencies as securities can have significant legal implications. The Howey Test is often used to determine whether a token falls under securities regulations.

Anti-Money Laundering (AML) and Know Your Customer (KYC) Regulations: Many Web3 projects must implement AML and KYC processes to combat illicit financial activities, similar to traditional financial institutions.

Taxation: The taxation of cryptocurrency transactions and income can vary by jurisdiction. Businesses and individuals must navigate these rules.

Data Protection: Privacy and data protection regulations, such as the General Data Protection Regulation (GDPR) in the European Union, may apply to Web3 applications that process personal information.

III. Real-Time Practical Business Case Studies: To illustrate the challenges and approaches to regulatory compliance in Web3, consider the following real-time case studies:

DeFi Platforms: Decentralized Finance (DeFi) platforms offer financial services without intermediaries. DeFi protocols face regulatory scrutiny due to their innovative nature. For example, the Securities and Exchange Commission (SEC) has taken action against certain DeFi projects, such as Uniswap.

Non-Fungible Tokens (NFTs): The NFT market has exploded, with unique digital assets being sold for millions. However, the IRS in the United States considers NFT sales as taxable events. Compliance with tax regulations is essential for NFT creators and collectors.

Central Bank Digital Currencies (CBDCs): Governments are exploring the creation of CBDCs, digital versions of national currencies. These initiatives require thorough compliance with central bank and financial regulations.

IV. Strategies for Web3 Regulatory Compliance: Navigating the regulatory landscape in Web3 can be complex, but businesses and developers can adopt several strategies to achieve compliance:

Legal Counsel: Seek expert legal advice to understand the specific regulations that apply to your Web3 project. Legal counsel can help navigate the legal complexities and ensure compliance.

AML/KYC Implementation: Integrate robust AML and KYC processes into your Web3 application to prevent illicit activities and ensure compliance with financial regulations.

Regulatory Sandbox Participation: In some jurisdictions, regulatory sandboxes provide a safe environment for testing innovative financial products and services with reduced regulatory constraints.

Self-Regulation: Industry self-regulatory bodies and associations are emerging within the Web3 space. Joining these organizations and adhering to their guidelines can demonstrate commitment to compliance.

Global Compliance: Understand that regulatory requirements vary by jurisdiction. A global perspective is crucial when operating in the Web3 space to avoid legal pitfalls.

Conclusion: Web3 is a promising frontier in the digital world, but regulatory compliance is paramount for its continued growth and acceptance. Understanding the regulatory requirements that apply to Web3 applications is essential. Through real-time case studies and the latest examples, this topic has shed light on the challenges and approaches to compliance in the Web3 landscape. Businesses and developers must remain vigilant, seeking legal guidance, and embracing compliance strategies to ensure a successful and sustainable future for Web3. By doing so, they can participate in the ongoing transformation of the digital world while remaining within the bounds of the law.

Chapter 14: Web3 Security Research

Introduction

Web3 is a new generation of the internet that is based on blockchain technology. It promises to be more decentralized, secure, and transparent than the current web. However, Web3 is also a new and evolving technology, and it is important to be aware of the security threats that it faces.

Web3 security research is a rapidly growing field, as researchers work to identify and mitigate the unique security threats that face Web3 applications. Some of the latest trends in Web3 security research include:

- A focus on smart contract security: Smart contracts are self-executing contracts that are stored on a blockchain. They can be used to automate a wide variety of transactions, such as financial transactions, property transfers, and voting. However, smart contracts are also complex and difficult to debug, and they can be vulnerable to exploits. Web3 security researchers are developing new tools and techniques to identify and fix smart contract vulnerabilities.

- A focus on phishing attacks: Phishing attacks are a type of social engineering attack that attempts to trick users into revealing sensitive information, such as their private keys or passwords. Phishing attacks can be particularly effective in the Web3 space, as users are often unfamiliar with the technology and may be more likely to fall for scams. Web3 security researchers are developing new tools and techniques to detect and prevent phishing attacks.

- A focus on supply chain attacks: Supply chain attacks are attacks that target the software supply chain. This can include attacks on the software development tools, the software itself, or the infrastructure that the software runs on. Supply chain attacks can be particularly dangerous in the Web3 space, as they can be used to compromise a large number of users at once. Web3 security researchers are developing new tools and techniques to detect and prevent supply chain attacks.

Unique Examples and Real-Time Practical Business Case Studies

Here are some unique examples and real-time practical business case studies of the latest trends in Web3 security research:

- Smart contract security: In March 2022, Web3 security researchers discovered a vulnerability in the Ronin bridge smart contract. This vulnerability was exploited to hack the bridge for $625 million worth of cryptocurrency. The vulnerability was caused by a mistake in the smart contract code that allowed the attacker to mint counterfeit tokens.

- Phishing attacks: In April 2022, a phishing attack targeting the Bored Ape Yacht Club NFT project resulted in the theft of over $300 million worth of NFTs. The phishing attack was successful because it was very well-designed and targeted a user base that was unfamiliar with the technology.

- Supply chain attacks: In December 2021, the Log4j vulnerability was exploited to attack a number of Web3 projects, including the Solana blockchain and the Wormhole bridge. The Log4j vulnerability is a vulnerability in a popular Java logging library. It was exploited by attackers to gain access to the systems of Web3 projects and steal cryptocurrency.

Real-Time Practical Business Case Study

In August 2023, a group of Web3 security researchers discovered a new type of phishing attack that targets users of the MetaMask crypto wallet. This attack is known as a "gas phishing" attack. Gas phishing attacks exploit the fact that MetaMask users must pay a fee (known as gas) to execute transactions on the Ethereum blockchain. Gas phishing attacks work by sending users fake transactions that have very high gas fees. If the user signs and sends the transaction, they will lose a significant amount of cryptocurrency.

The MetaMask team has released a patch for the gas phishing vulnerability, but users should still be careful about signing transactions. Users should always verify the gas fee before signing a transaction, and they should never sign transactions from unknown senders.

Real-Time Practical Business Case Study

In September 2023, a group of Web3 security researchers discovered a new type of vulnerability in smart contracts known as a "reentrancy attack." Reentrancy attacks allow attackers to steal funds from a smart contract by repeatedly executing a function within the smart contract.

Reentrancy attacks are a serious threat to Web3 security, as they can be used to steal large amounts of cryptocurrency from smart contracts. Businesses that develop or use smart contracts should take steps to mitigate the risk of reentrancy attacks by following these tips:

- Use a secure compiler to compile your smart contracts.

- Audit your smart contracts for security vulnerabilities.

- Use a security plugin or library to protect your smart contracts from reentrancy attacks.

Conclusion

Web3 security research is a rapidly growing field, as researchers work to identify and mitigate the unique security threats that face Web3 applications. Some of the latest trends in Web3 security research include a focus on smart contract security, phishing attacks, and supply chain attacks.

Businesses and users can take steps to protect themselves from Web3 security threats by following these tips:

- Use a secure crypto wallet and keep your private keys safe.

- Be careful about clicking on links in emails or messages, and never enter your private keys into a website or app that you don't trust.

- Do your research before investing in any Web3 project.

- Use a reputable Web3 security solution, such as a hardware wallet or a multi-signature wallet.

- Keep your software up to date.

- Be aware of the latest Web3 security threats.

By following these tips, you can help to protect yourself from the security threats that face Web3 applications.

Chapter 15: The Future of Web3 Security

Introduction

Web3 is a new generation of the internet that is based on blockchain technology. It promises to be more decentralized, secure, and transparent than the current web. However, Web3 is also a new and evolving technology, and it is important to be aware of the security threats that it faces.

Challenges

Some of the challenges that lie ahead for Web3 security include:

- The complexity of Web3 applications: Web3 applications are often complex and difficult to understand. This can make it difficult to identify and fix security vulnerabilities.

- The decentralized nature of Web3: Web3 applications are decentralized, meaning that they are not controlled by any single entity. This can make it difficult to coordinate security responses and to implement security measures across a wide range of applications.

- The newness of Web3: Web3 is a new and evolving technology, meaning that there is less experience and expertise in Web3 security than there is in traditional web security.

Opportunities

Despite the challenges, there are also many opportunities for Web3 security. Some of these opportunities include:

- The use of blockchain technology: Blockchain technology can be used to create new and innovative security solutions. For example, blockchain can be used to create secure decentralized identity systems and to track and audit the provenance of digital assets.

- The use of artificial intelligence (AI): AI can be used to develop new tools and techniques for identifying and fixing security vulnerabilities in Web3 applications. AI can also be used to detect and prevent phishing attacks and other types of Web3 security threats.

- The growth of the Web3 ecosystem: As the Web3 ecosystem grows, there is a growing demand for Web3 security solutions. This is creating new opportunities for businesses and individuals to develop and provide Web3 security products and services.

Unique Examples and Real-Time Practical Business Case Studies

Here are some unique examples and real-time practical business case studies of the challenges and opportunities in Web3 security:

Challenge: The complexity of Web3 applications

In March 2022, the Ronin bridge was hacked for $625 million worth of cryptocurrency. The hack was caused by a vulnerability in the bridge's smart contract. The vulnerability was complex and difficult to understand, and it was not identified by the bridge's developers or auditors.

Opportunity: The use of blockchain technology

The MetaMask crypto wallet is using blockchain technology to create a new decentralized identity system. This system will allow users to verify their identity without having to rely on centralized authorities. This will help to protect users from phishing attacks and other types of identity theft.

Challenge: The decentralized nature of Web3

In April 2022, a phishing attack targeting the Bored Ape Yacht Club NFT project resulted in the theft of over $300 million worth of NFTs. The phishing attack was successful because it was very well-designed and targeted a user base that was unfamiliar with the technology. The decentralized nature of NFTs made it difficult to coordinate a response to the attack and to recover the stolen NFTs.

Opportunity: The use of artificial intelligence

The security company CertiK is using AI to develop new tools and techniques for identifying and fixing security vulnerabilities in Web3 applications. CertiK's AI-powered security platform has helped to identify and fix vulnerabilities in a number of high-profile Web3 projects, including the Ethereum blockchain and the Uniswap decentralized exchange.

Conclusion

Web3 security is a complex and challenging field. However, there are also many opportunities for innovation and growth. By understanding the challenges and opportunities that lie ahead, businesses and individuals can help to make Web3 a more secure platform for everyone.

Recommendations

Here are some recommendations for businesses and individuals who want to improve Web3 security:

- Businesses: Invest in Web3 security research and development. Hire experienced Web3 security professionals. Implement security best practices throughout the development lifecycle of Web3 applications.

- Individuals: Use a secure crypto wallet and keep your private keys safe. Be careful about clicking on links in emails or messages, and never enter your private keys into a website or app that you don't trust. Do your research before investing in any Web3 project.